Love is The Meaning

Ann Lewin is an accomplished poet and is in much demand as a retreat leader.

She taught RE and English for many years and was later Welfare Advisor for International Students at the University of Southampton. She has also helped in the training of ordinands at Sarum College.

Her other published titles are *Watching for the Kingfisher* (Canterbury Press) and *Words By the Way* (Inspire).

Every good wish

Ann Lewin

Love is
The Meaning

*Growing in Faith with
Julian of Norwich*

Ann Lewin

CANTERBURY
PRESS
Norwich

© Ann Lewin 2006 and 2010

This edition published in 2010 by the
Canterbury Press Norwich
Editorial office
13–17 Long Lane,
London, EC1A 9PN, UK

Canterbury Press is an imprint of Hymns Ancient and
Modern Ltd (a registered charity)
13A Hellesdon Park Road, Norwich,
Norfolk, NR6 5DR, UK

First published under the title *Growing in Love* by Inspire,
an imprint of the Methodist Publishing House, in 2006

www.scm-canterburypress.co.uk

British Library Cataloguing in Publication data

A catalogue record for this book is available
from the British Library

978 1 84825 050 5

Printed and bound in Great Britain by
CPI Antony Rowe, Chippenham SN14 6LH

Contents

Preface

Love was his meaning. That simple sentence sums up the insights Julian of Norwich gained through her experience described in *The Revelation of Divine Love*. The purpose of this book is to encourage readers to explore some of those insights, and help them to fulfil Julian's hope that, as a result of thinking about her experience, their love for God will grow.

The Introduction sets Julian in her context, and describes her life as an anchoress and the event which led to her writing about her experience. The book is constructed so that each chapter then provides material for study in groups, perhaps during Lent.

Chapter 1 starts from Julian's vision of the hazelnut, and her realization that everything that exists has its being because God loves it. How can we hold fast to that truth about God and the world in the midst of natural disasters, and those caused by human behaviour? What part does intercession play in helping God's kingdom to be established on earth?

Chapter 2 concentrates on an exploration of the nature of God. Julian said, 'As truly as God is our Father, so also is God our Mother'. How does the imagery we use affect our understanding of God's nature? How does Julian's imagery free us to explore imagery which may speak freshly to our world?

Chapter 3 concentrates on prayer as the expression of our relationship with our Father/Mother God. What do we do when prayer goes dead? We look at Julian's insistence that we should persevere, and seek God who alone can satisfy our longing.

Chapter 4 deals with sin, the barrier that we put between ourselves and God. Can we believe that nothing we do stops God loving us? We discuss the problem of inappropriate guilt, and failing to accept that we are forgiven.

Chapter 5 looks at Julian's conviction that all shall be well. How can we believe that when so much around us seems to indicate the opposite? What do we make of suffering?

Each chapter concludes with some questions which might be helpful in stimulating discussion, though the material may lead readers in a different direction. If the book is being used for group study, ideally everyone in the group should have a copy of the book, so that the relevant chapter can be read before each meeting. But in order to facilitate participation by people who have not been able to prepare in this way, it would be helpful for one person to spend about 15 minutes at the start of a meeting introducing the material for study. This introduction should be followed by 15 minutes for individual reflection on the material. Where people are not used to taking part in group discussion, it is helpful to suggest that at the end of the time of reflection, participants spend a few minutes talking with another member of the group about anything which has struck them as significant, or about which they would like further information. The discussion can then be opened up to the whole group. The questions at the end of each chapter are intended to be used as a stimulus – the material may stimulate discussion without recourse to the questions, but it is worth noting that the questions imply that some action as a result of discussion is desirable. Each chapter ends with a suggestion for a time of worship, which should last about 10 minutes.

People who use the material on their own may find it helpful to link up with another person to discuss what they have read and thought about.

At the end of the book there is material that might be used in a Eucharist based on Julian's words, and some suggestions for further reading.

Ann Lewin
November 2006

Acknowledgements

I am grateful to all the people who have shared the exploration of Julian's writings with me, through Julian Groups, conversations or the written word; to Gary Philbrick who read the manuscript at an early stage, and commented helpfully on it, and to Canterbury Press for re-publishing the book.

We gratefully acknowledge the use of copyright items for which permission has been given by:

The Revd Fr Superior of the Community of the Resurrection, Mirfield, for the prayer written by W. H. Frere, quoted in chapter 3;

The Estate of the late John V. Taylor, for the quotations from *The Christlike God*, SCM Press 1992 quoted in Chapter 4;

All quotations from Julian's writings are taken from *Julian of Norwich Showings* in the Classics of Western Spirituality series, published in 1978 by the Paulist Press, Inc., New York, Mahwah, N.J. Used with permission. www.paulistpress.com

Introduction

The Revelation of Divine Love, the book written by Julian of Norwich, remained almost unknown for centuries after her death. No one knows its true history, but detective work by scholars suggests that her original manuscript was copied and found its way into one or more of the monastic libraries of the time. At the time of the Reformation, when the monasteries were dissolved and their riches dispersed, a copy of the book must have been taken to one of the mother houses on the continent. By the 1660s there was a copy in the Bibliothèque Nationale in Paris. An English Benedictine monk named Serenus de Cressy, who was chaplain to a convent in Paris, asked his Abbot for permission to publish a version of the book, and in 1670 the first ever printed edition of *The Revelation* was produced.

The event passed almost unnoticed, and it was 200 years before the book took another step on its road to becoming a bestseller. Sir Hans Sloane bought the Manor of Chelsea in 1712 to set up a botanic garden. He was a great collector, and acquired many collections made by other people too. These became the foundation of the British Museum when he left everything to the nation on his death in 1753, in exchange for £20,000 to be paid to his executors by Parliament. Among the manuscripts were two copies of Julian's book, but it was another hundred years before the Revd Henry Collins brought out a printed edition of *The Revelation* from one of the Sloane manuscripts. Serenus de Cressy's edition had been reprinted in 1843. There is no record of how well either of them sold, but we do know that Florence Nightingale took a copy with her to Scutari Hospital in the Crimea. In 1901, the publishers Methuen brought out another edition of *The Revelation*, edited by a woman called Grace Warrack who came from Edinburgh, and who died in 1932. Nothing more is known of her than her name – in that respect she is very like Julian. But her work was an instant success, and was reprinted time and again during the next 70 years – it was never out of print even through two world wars. There are many editions of Julian's work now, translated from Julian's Chaucerian language into modern English.

Julian lived from 1342 to about 1420, a period of history which had its share of troubles. Edward III came to power in 1330, after a series of intrigues involving his mother Isabella and her lover, Mortimer, who had taken the throne from Edward's father. Mortimer was put to death, but Isabella was allowed her freedom, which she enjoyed at the expense of those who lived near her residences, one of which was at Castle Rising, near Kings Lynn. Her upkeep was quite a drain on Norfolk resources. Edward was a good soldier and a popular hero, but his desire for battle caused another drain on resources as men went off to fight the French and the Scots at the beginning of what was later called the Hundred Years' War.

When Julian was about six the Black Death began in Dorset, and six months later, in January 1349, it reached Norfolk. A contemporary witness described how the disease was so contagious that anyone who touched the sick or dying caught it, so that the priests were buried in the same graves as those to whom they had ministered. Half the clergy in Norwich died in that and subsequent outbreaks.

Cattle disease and a series of bad harvests compounded the situation. People were starving, taxation was heavy, the feudal lords tried to keep wages low, leaving people in poverty. In 1381 the Peasants' Revolt led by Wat Tyler and Jack Straw began in Kent, and spread throughout the country. In East Anglia there was much resentment against the great landowners, the churches and the monasteries. Bishop Despenser of Norwich was largely responsible for restoring order in the area, but he used fairly ruthless methods. Although people were grateful to him for acting decisively, they were also aware that he had contributed to the discontent by sharing in the extravagance of the royal household which had caused the high taxation in the first place. And talking of bishops, it was also around this time that there were two Popes claiming power, Clement in Avignon and Urban in Rome engaging in theological slanging matches.

John Wyclif, an Oxford scholar and preacher, was one of many who attacked abuses in the church, but he himself was condemned, and eventually retired to Lutterworth where he and his fellow Lollards devoted themselves to promoting the availability of the Scriptures in English. The first complete translation of the Bible in English appeared in 1390, three years before Julian's *Revelation* was written.

That was the background to Julian's life. Who was she? We don't know much detail. We know she was born in 1342, and it is suggested that she was educated by nuns at Carrow just outside Norwich. She said herself that she was unlettered, though that may only have meant that she didn't understand Latin very well. We know that she lived much of her life as an anchoress in a cell attached to St Julian's Church in Norwich, but we don't know her real name. It was the custom for anchoresses to take their name from the church where they served.

Anchoresses were women who lived a solitary life in the middle of a town or village. Like the Desert Fathers and Mothers before them, they withdrew from normal social life, in order to grow to love God more. But they were not entirely divorced from the world around them. Their prayers for the place where they lived, and the advice they gave to those who came seeking counsel were invaluable. Julian would have lived by a simple rule based on the Benedictine pattern of prayer, work and rest. We don't know which specific Rule Julian followed, but apart from Benedict's Rule, there would have been two main influences on her way of life. One was the rule which Aelred of Rievaulx had written for his anchoress sister in about 1160 and the other was the *Ancrene Riwle*, written early in the thirteenth century for three sisters who lived a contemplative life. Since she was enclosed in her cell, she would have had a servant to do the shopping and various household chores: Alice and Sara were two successive servants named in bequests made to Julian. And the Rule allowed her to have a cat – not for cosy domestic reasons, but to deal with vermin.

Julian's daily life would have been punctuated by times of prayer. The cathedral clock would have helped her to order her day, and the bells of nearby churches and religious houses would have called her to recollection alongside those living the monastic hours nearby. This framework would have followed the Benedictine order of seven 'hours' of formal prayer each day: Matins just after midnight, Lauds just before dawn, followed by Prime, Terce at 9 a.m., Sext at noon, None at 3 p.m., Vespers in the early evening, and Compline at bedtime. Fixed prayers would have been said at those times, based on Psalms, Paternosters (The Lord's Prayer), and Aves (the Hail Mary). Julian would have been able to hear the parish priest saying his 'Hours' in the church next to her cell, but her Rule would not have encouraged her to join in, even if her Latin had enabled her to. This framework was intended to support her own prayer, which would have included times for reading and reflection. It assumes that there would have been periods when Julian would not have been available to listen to people or give advice.

Julian's cell would have had two windows, one into the church so that she could hear Mass and receive Communion, the other onto the main road from the city centre to the port. Through this window she would have spoken to those who came to her for advice. She didn't record the names of her visitors, but we know from another source of one well-known person who came. Margery Kempe, who lived in Bishop's (now King's) Lynn, in Norfolk, records in her own book that she visited Julian for advice. Margery was a devout woman who experienced the presence of Christ very vividly, in ways that often caused her to weep uncontrollably. This 'gift of tears' was a well-known phenomenon in medieval times, recognized as coming from God. That did not prevent people around them from finding those who had the gift rather an embarrassment. Margery could not cry quietly, and sometimes drowned out the preacher's words in church, which others found annoying. She came to ask Julian for advice and affirmation, which Julian readily gave her after hearing Margery describe how her gift affected her. Julian was convinced that the gift was genuine, and assured Margery that God did not give the gift to unstable people, so she did not need to fear that she was mad, as people sometimes suggested. Margery writes of the consolation she had from conversation with Julian over several days.[1]

Julian would also have been aware of the traffic passing her window on the way to and from the port – signs of prosperity and economic growth consequent on the war. The ports of the south coast were too close to France for comfort and safety. Norwich, linked by roads and waterways to London, York and Lincoln, was in a key position for wool and cloth trades. All the religious orders established houses in Norwich too, so it was a centre for the exchange of ideas as well as goods.

We don't know when Julian became an anchoress, but we do know that when she was thirty and a half she had the most extraordinary experience. For years Julian had prayed for singleness of heart and deeper devotion in three ways:

> I desired three graces by the gift of God. The first was to have a recollection of Christ's Passion. The second was a bodily sickness, and the third was to have, of God's gift, three wounds. As to the first, it came to my mind with devotion; it seemed to me that I had great feeling for the Passion of Christ, but I

still desired to have more by the grace of God. I thought that I wished that I had been at that time with Mary Magdalen and with the others who were Christ's lovers, so that I might have seen with my own eyes our Lord's Passion which he suffered for me, so that I might have suffered with him as others did who loved him .... As to the second grace, there came into my mind with contrition – a free gift of God which I did not seek – a desire of my will to have by God's gift a bodily sickness, and I wished it to be so severe that it might seem mortal, so that I should in that sickness receive all the rites which Holy Church had to give me, whilst I myself should believe that I was dying, and everyone who saw me would think the same, for I wanted no comfort from any human, earthly life. In this sickness I wanted to have every kind of pain, bodily and spiritual, which I should have if I were dying, every fear, and assault from devils, and every other kind of pain except the departure of the spirit, for I hoped that this would be profitable to me when I should die, because I desired soon to be with my God.

I desired these two, concerning the Passion and sickness, with a condition, because it seemed to me that neither was an ordinary petition, and therefore I said: Lord, you know what I want. If it be your will that I have it, grant it to me, and if it be not your will, good Lord, do not be displeased, for I want nothing which you do not want. When I was young I desired to have that sickness when I was thirty years old. As to the third, I heard a man of Holy Church tell the story of St Cecilia, and from his explanation I understood that she received three wounds in the neck from a

sword, through which she suffered death.
Moved by this, I conceived a great desire, and
prayed our Lord God that he would grant me
in the course of my life three wounds, that is,
the wound of contrition, the wound of
compassion, and the wound of longing with
my will for God. Just as I asked for the other
two conditionally, I asked for this third
without any condition. The two desires which
I mentioned first passed from my mind, and
the third remained there continually.
(ST Ch 1)

We might think that none of these was an ordinary
petition. The first was for an understanding of the passion
of Christ. This was not just for intellectual knowledge –
Julian was writing as many medieval poets and spiritual
writers did, in accord with the biblical tradition
expounded by Jesus in the Gospels (Matthew 16.24ff;
Mark 8.34ff; Luke 9.23ff) and by Paul (Philippians 3.10–
11) that to enter fully into life with Christ, we have to share
in some way in his sufferings.

The second petition was a request for a kind of dress
rehearsal for death. This perhaps seems bizarre to us, for
whom illness and death are to be avoided at all costs. But
we need to see it in the context of medieval spirituality
which had a strong sense of the importance of coming to
terms with death: to know that you are going to die
enables you to live with more awareness. This was not a
neurotic preoccupation – as with the first prayer, she
made it very clear that she was praying for a gift, and if it
was not forthcoming, then she would take that to be God's
will.

The third prayer for the three 'wounds', as she called
them, of contrition, loving compassion, and the longing of
the will for God, sprang from her belief that only when
desire for God had penetrated into her very being would
there be true growth in love.

When Julian was thirty and a half, she became seriously ill. She received the Last Rites of the Church, and progressively weakened. On the third night a priest was sent for, and he held a crucifix in front of her, so that she could gaze on it to the end. Suddenly, she said,

> In that moment, my pain left me, and I was as sound as ever I was before or since. (ST Ch 1)

She still thought she was going to die; in fact her mother, who was with her, thought that she had died, and reached out to close her eyes. But instead of dying, Julian actually had her first prayer answered, and in a series of extraordinary visions experienced the Passion of Christ. It was a very vivid experience:

> Suddenly I saw red blood running down from under the crown, hot and flowing freely and copiously, a living stream, just as it was at the time when the crown of thorns was thrust upon his blessed head.
> (LT Ch 4)

Julian expected to see Jesus die, but as she continued to gaze at the crucifix, she saw his body change, much as her own body had recovered, and he began to speak to her, through 15 brief visions linked to aspects of his Passion, extending her understanding of God and of her own need. When these experiences ended, she began to be assailed by the devil in all his medieval imagery – heat, foul smell, muttering in her ears – and it has been suggested that perhaps at this point in her illness she was given medicinal herbs which caused hallucinations. At one stage, Julian wondered whether she was going mad, but the priest who was ministering to her assured her, when she described what was happening, that this was not madness but an experience from God.

Julian recorded her visions almost immediately, in what is known as the Short Text (ST) of *The Revelation of Divine Love*. Then she spent 20 years or so mulling over

her experience, and produced what is called the Long Text
(LT) in 1393. Julian is the first writer known to be a
woman writing in the vernacular. (Chaucer was a
contemporary.) She became convinced that the value of
her experience lay not in the fact that she had had the
visions, but that the experience had helped her to love God
more, and it was to help others to love God more that she
eventually shared all that she had learned:

> I am not good because of the revelations, but
> only if I love God better, and inasmuch as you
> love God better, it is more to you than to me.
> (LT Ch 9)

She was diffident about conveying the insights she had
for, as she said,

> I am a woman, ignorant, weak and frail
> (ST Ch 6)

and women were not expected to take a leading role in
talking about matters of faith. But she was so sure that she
had to pass on what she had come to understand that she
overcame this fear, and by writing in the vernacular,
risking association with the Lollards who were frequently
executed not far from her cell, she made her insights
available to all her fellow Christians. This reflection, in
fact, became the answer to her third prayer, which was for
the wounds of true contrition, loving compassion, and a
longing for the will of God to sink deep into her.

Julian's description of the Passion of Christ does not
immediately appeal to modern taste – it is brutal and gory,
as was much contemporary art. Early portrayals of Christ
had concentrated on his victory over death. Crucifixion
was a shameful death, and the thought of portraying Jesus
who was God as well as man suffering and dying was
unacceptable. It took a few centuries for the arguments
about the true nature of Christ to come to the point where
theologians could accept that portraying the suffering of
Christ in his human form did not detract from his divine

nature. Medieval art sometimes took that to extremes, perhaps mirroring people's experience, and portraying Christ as one who entered fully into the suffering of humanity.

The reason why Julian's work has become one of the classics of the literature of spirituality lies in the insights that flowed from her experience, insights that many people have found liberating and helpful whenever the state of the world or of human nature has seemed overwhelming, when imagery for God has appeared constricting, or when prayer has gone dead.

It is a selection of these insights which form the basis for study and reflection.

Note

1.   *The Book of Margery Kempe*, Penguin 1985, Chapter 18, pp. 77ff.

1

Coping with Troubled Times

'I don't know what the world is coming to.' That is often our instinctive response as we look at the news on television, or read the paper, or hear about yet another disaster somewhere in the world. We live, as Julian did, in troubled times. But troubled times have always been part of the background to our existence.

Peter the Monk, writing in 1274, is reported to have said, giving his view of contemporary society:

> The world is passing through troubled times. The young people of today think of nothing but themselves. They have no reverence for parents or old age. They are impatient of all restraint. They talk as if they knew everything, and what passes as wisdom with us is foolishness with them. As for the girls, they are foolish and immoderate in speech, behaviour and dress.[1]

Aristotle made a similar comment when he said,

> When I look at the younger generation, I despair of the future of civilization.[2]

But it isn't only the younger generation which gives cause for concern. Going back still further, the Psalms are full of the same kind of recognition that the world is not as God intended it to be, and they also give us a model for approaching the tensions we experience as we live in our own times. The Psalmist doesn't try to pretend that everything is in control: he pours out his anguish at the state of the world, and alongside it sets his belief that ultimately God is the rock on whom we depend, and that God's faithfulness is to be trusted.

We need to remind ourselves of that faithfulness. One of the first truths Julian became aware of in her experience of God was that everything that exists is held in the love of God which wraps us around, like our clothing. She had a vision of a hazelnut lying in the palm of her hand, and as she puzzled over what the vision meant, she realized that her concern for its fragility was misplaced. 'It is', she wrote, 'because God loves it. And thus everything has being through the love of God.'

> I saw that he is to us everything which is good and comforting for our help. He is our clothing, who wraps us round and enfolds us for love, embraces us and shelters us, surrounds us for his love, which is so tender that he may never desert us. And so in this sight I saw that he is everything which is good, as I understand.
>
> And in this he showed me something small, no bigger than a hazelnut, lying in the palm of my hand, as it seemed to me, and it was as round as a ball. I looked at it with the eye of my understanding and thought: What can this be? I was amazed that it could last, for I thought because of its littleness it would suddenly have fallen into nothing. And I was answered in my understanding: It lasts and always will, because God loves it; and thus everything has being through the love of God. (LT Ch 5)

This was no cosy 'God's in his heaven, all's right with the world'3 avoidance of what was going on around her, but a basic attitude of trust which she brought to bear in all her thinking about the world and the lives of individuals.

We need constantly to remind ourselves of God's faithfulness. But how can we hold fast to that truth about the world and God when faced with the obscenities caused by human behaviour, when war and terrorism are the headlines, and our screens are full of heartrending pictures of suffering caused by famine and poverty which could have been avoided; when we see people's lives being destroyed by the power of oppressors; or when the world itself seems to turn against us, and natural disasters strike with the force of a tsunami?

As the Psalmist encourages us to do, we have to learn to set our belief that God is God, alongside all that we watch or hear, and hold fast to the truth that this is a world which God loves, and that God holds everything in existence. But we can't stop there. Julian said that God makes us partners in the work of establishing his will:

> [God] teaches us to pray and to have firm
> trust that we shall have what we pray for,
> because everything which is done would be
> done, even though we had never prayed for it.
> But God's love is so great that he regards us as
> partners in his good work, and so he moves us
> to pray for what it pleases him to do....
> (ST Ch 19)

This way of praying is what we call Intercession, a familiar part of many acts of worship, and the *raison d'être* of many prayer groups. When we pray in this way, we remember that when God looked at the world he had made, he saw that it was very good. We share God's anguish that when he looks at the world now, he weeps to see what has become of it, and in effect we say to God, we love your world too, and long for it to be what you intended it to be from the beginning. Intercession is not a matter of handing everything over to God for God to sort out, it is a way of praying that states our intention of putting our energy alongside God's energy in transforming the world into God's kingdom of justice, peace and wholeness.

But we can't pray as though the world is something apart from us. We are part of the problem, as well as being potentially part of the solution. Everything that we do or say or think is either an expression of our commitment to God's will, or our lack of it. Intercession requires penitence, the recognition that we have a share in what is wrong with the world. We are not the 'goodies' who have got everything right, praying for the 'baddies' who haven't. Rather, we are people who recognize that the fault-line runs through each one of us. Only if we have never had unkind thoughts about our neighbours could we ever claim otherwise. 'Lord, have mercy' is a prayer we all need to pray for ourselves as well as others.

And that can help us when we consider Jesus' command to love our enemies and pray for those who abuse us (Luke 6.27–28; Matthew 5.44–45). We find it easy enough to pray for people in need of any kind. We want their health and happiness to be restored. But to pray for terrorists and murderers? We perhaps find that requirement a step too far. It is helpful to recognize that to pray for someone does not mean that we approve of what they are or how they behave. Our prayer is that God will penetrate their hearts and minds with his light and love, and bring them to understand that there are better ways than the ones they have chosen to bring about a kingdom where people really do honour one another and seek the common good.

Julian perhaps knew the advice given to his sister by Aelred of Rievaulx:

> Embrace the whole world with the arms of
> your love, and in that act at once consider and
> congratulate the good, contemplate and
> mourn over the wicked. In that act look upon
> the afflicted and oppressed and feel
> compassion for them. In that act call to mind
> the wretchedness of the poor, the groans of
> orphans, the abandonment of widows, the

gloom of the sorrowful, the needs of travellers,
the prayers of virgins, the perils of those at
sea, the temptations of monks, the
responsibilities of prelates, the labours of
those waging war. In your love take them all
to your heart, weep over them, offer your
prayers for them.[4]

That way of life, of course, involves us in change too.
Intercession is not just what we say, it is what we do as a
result of our prayer: it really begins when our time of
prayer ends. It can be quite a dangerous way of praying,
because we may hear God say to us, 'And what are you
going to do about the situation?' We won't all be called to
go out to troubled places to work for peace. But we all have
our part to play in showing our commitment to a better
world. Writing letters to MPs, and asking questions of
those who have power to change policies is part of
intercession. So at a different level is sending messages of
support to those who suffer – the 'Get Well' cards for the
sick and the postcards to political prisoners are all part of
our living the gospel.

So, if we are working with God by our prayer in action,
why hasn't the world changed all that much in its human
relationships through the centuries? Is it because we
haven't prayed hard enough? Surely not. God makes us
partners in his work of transforming the world, but he
doesn't force us to work with him. The reason why our
prayer and our action don't always bring the desired effect
could well be that there are too many other people
blocking the way and obstructing God's will.

The events of the Holocaust are sometimes cited to
demonstrate God's powerlessness. Millions of Jews must
have prayed for deliverance: why did God not act to save
his chosen race? Perhaps the answer lies in the location of
political power at the time. However much God willed to
spare his people, the forces working for their
extermination were set powerfully against God. The

problem lies not so much in thinking of God as powerless, as in the way that people use their free will. Ultimately, of course, God is responsible for giving us free will in the first place. But if God had not done so, the whole human story would have been different, and our questions, if we were free to question, would have been different too.

There is no simple answer to the question of apparently unanswered prayer. But to an allied question about where God is in the situations which bring us to despair, Julian gives us a clue. God's love is always to be found manifesting itself somewhere. In the death camps of the Holocaust, God's love was shown in the selflessness with which some people took the place of those who were on their way to the gas chambers. God's love was shown in the way people took risks to save the lives of Jews – Schindler with his List[5] was only one of those who used their position to provide papers to enable Jews to find freedom. Julian says that the answer to her question about God's intentions is that his meaning was love.

> I was taught that love is our Lord's meaning. And I saw very certainly in this and in everything that before God made us he loved us, which love was never abated and never will be. And in this love he has done all his works, and in this love he has made all things profitable to us, and in this love our life is everlasting.
> (LT Ch 86)

Some questions to ponder

1. Does Julian's vision of the hazelnut help us to understand God's faithfulness?

2. What areas of political life would we be prepared to question in the light of the gospel?

3. Is there a letter you would like to write to anyone in authority about an area of public life?

4. Does what we have been considering this week offer any guidance to people compiling intercessions for use in church?

Notes

1. Information from the internet: http://www.edges.tv

2. http://www.edges.tv

3. Robert Browning, *Pippa Passes*, PT 1, 222ff.

4. *The Works of Aelred of Rievaulx, Vol 1, A Rule of Life for a Recluse Part II The inner man Treatises*, Cistercian Publications, Spencer, Massachusetts 1971.

5. Thomas Kenneally, *Schindler's Ark 1982*. Filmed by Steven Spielberg as *Schindler's List*.

Suggestion for worship at the end of the session

Settle to stillness, using music or a hymn.

Our Father, God almighty, is full of strength and goodness, in him we have our being:
**We come to God our Father with confidence,
for our fragmented lives to be knit together again.**
As truly as God is our Father, so is also God our Mother, full of wisdom, tenderness and love:
**To God our Mother we come with confidence,
to be restored in love.**
God is also the Holy Spirit, active in us through grace, praying through us and enabling us to yield ourselves to God:
**To God the Holy Spirit we come with confidence,
to be opened to God's grace.**
God the Trinity is strength and goodness,
Wisdom, tenderness and love, who never leaves us:
**God, of your goodness, give us yourself,
for if we ask anything which is less
we shall always be in want.
Only in you we have all.**

Time for reflection on some words from Mother Julian

God teaches us to pray and to have a firm trust that we shall have what we pray for, because everything which is done would be done, even though we had never prayed for it. But God's love is so great that he regards us as partners in his good work, and so he moves us to pray for what it pleases him to do.

Prayer for the world and for ourselves

In the places of decision-making,
and the places of powerlessness:
Come, Lord, **hold us in your love, and heal us.**

In the places of wealth,
and the places of poverty:
Come, Lord, **hold us in your love, and heal us.**

Where we are healthy,
and where we are sick:
Come, Lord, **hold us in your love, and heal us.**

Where people are oppressed,
and in the hearts of oppressors:
Come, Lord, **hold us in your love, and heal us.**

In the streets of plenty,
and in the dark corners and alleys:
Come, Lord, **hold us in your love, and heal us.**

In our places of worship,
and where there is no faith:
Come, Lord, **hold us in your love, and heal us.**

In our places of learning,
and in the depths of our ignorance:
Come, Lord, **hold us in your love, and heal us.**

In our homes and our welcomes, and where people
couldn't care less:
Come, Lord, **hold us in your love, and heal us.**

Blessing

God's great goodness fills all his creatures
and all his blessed works full,
and endlessly overflows in them;
for he is everlastingness,
and he made us only for himself,
and restored us by his precious Passion.
May he always preserve us in his blessed love,
and all this of his goodness. **Amen.**

We go in the peace of Christ. **Amen.**

2

The Nature of God

How do we think of this God who holds us in love? How do we address God? By what imagery do we describe God?

'Father' is the most usual description used in Christian circles. Many people, though, still carry within them a concept often portrayed pictorially in people's homes in Victorian times, of the All Seeing Eye of God, looking at everything that he had made and disapproving of most of it. That picture owes a great deal to some of the descriptions of God and his actions in the Old Testament. God seems to be rather unpredictable in the records of Jewish history. At times God is described as tender and loving, at others he is a terrible avenger. If we find ourselves rather confused by this, it is perhaps because we haven't grasped the idea that the Old Testament is the record of people's struggles to understand God and the circumstances of their lives. At times, perhaps, their idea of God is really a projection of what they would like to do themselves. When plans are thwarted, it is very tempting to think about destroying whoever it is who has caused the obstruction. The Psalmist's 'Break their teeth, O God' (Psalm 58.6) was perhaps not so much a prediction of how God would act, as a description of the Psalmist's own fantasy about what he would do if he were God. We are quite good at telling God how to go about things.

The idea of an avenging God is perpetuated in our time by the language of insurance companies which decline to accept liability for events which they describe as Acts of God. These are never pleasant events. The term is reserved for some very unpleasant occurrences – tsunamis, floods or earthquakes. And a common question when anything goes wrong is to say, 'What have I done to deserve this?' as though disasters or unpleasant occurrences are sent by a

God who is out to get us, rather than a God whose meaning is love.

But that is not the God who revealed himself in Jesus. Jesus described God as a parent passionately engaged with his children. Look at the imagery Luke uses in chapter 15 of his Gospel, when he describes God's relationship with his creation. Inanimate object, animal or son, God will go to any lengths to recover the lost. And it is in that context that Jesus said: 'When you pray, say "Our Father".' That was not the most frequently used imagery for God in the Scriptures Jesus had been brought up with – in the Old Testament God is often described as a King or a Judge, with a distinctly punitive edge to his character. Jesus picked up a softer side to God, and gave us another image to play with. The trouble is, we have got stuck with it, and sometimes find it difficult to move away from it to other imagery which might bring our relationship with God to life in a new way.

Julian used another parental image to describe God, when she suggested that we might refer to God as Mother.

> As truly as God is our Father, so truly is God our Mother, and he revealed that in everything, and especially in these sweet words where he says: I am he, that is to say: I am he, the power and goodness of fatherhood; I am he, the wisdom and lovingness of motherhood; I am he, the light and the grace which is all blessed love; I am he, the Trinity; I am he, the unity; I am he, the great supreme goodness of every kind of thing; I am he who makes you to love; I am he who makes you to long; I am he, the endless fulfilling of all true desires ...

and

> From this it follows that as truly as God is our Father, so truly is God our Mother. Our Father

wills, our Mother works, our good Lord the
Holy Spirit confirms. And therefore it is our
part to love our God in whom we have our
being, reverently thanking and praising him
for our creation, mightily praying to our
Mother for mercy and pity, and to our Lord
the Holy Spirit for help and grace. (LT Ch 59)

Julian picked up the feminine imagery, but she did not
substitute it for other imagery. She wrote consistently
about God as Trinity: she was not suggesting that God
could be reduced to one particular understanding of his
nature. God is always greater than anything we can
imagine.

Thinking of the maternal attributes of God was not new
even in Julian's day – it is there in the imagery of the Old
Testament: 'Underneath are the everlasting arms'
(Deuteronomy 33.27) is but one of many maternal images.
Hosea offers us another: 'It was I who taught Ephraim to
walk, I took them up in my arms; but they did not know
that I healed them ... I was to them like those who lift
infants to their cheeks. I bent down to them and fed them
(Hosea 11.3–4). Jesus picked up the maternal idea when
he said of Jerusalem: 'How often have I desired to gather
your children together as a hen gathers her brood under
her wings, and you were not willing!' (Matthew 23.37).
Anselm, Archbishop of Canterbury in the eleventh
century, used the same imagery in his well-known
canticle, with its refrain:

> *Gather your little ones to you, o God,*
> *as a hen gathers her brood to protect them.*

> Jesus, as a mother you gather your people to you,
> you are gentle with us as a mother with her children.

> Often you weep over our sins and our pride,
> tenderly you draw us from hatred and judgement.

You comfort us in sorrow and bind up our wounds,
in sickness you nurse us and with pure milk you feed
    us.

Jesus, by your dying we are born to new life,
by your anguish and labour we come forth in joy.

Despair turns to hope through your great goodness,
through your gentleness we find comfort in fear.

Your warmth gives life to the dead,
your touch makes sinners righteous.

Lord Jesus, in your mercy heal us,
in your love and tenderness remake us.

In your compassion bring grace and forgiveness,
for the beauty of heaven may your love prepare us.

Gather your little ones to you, o God,
as a hen gathers her brood to protect them.

It is worth spending some time thinking about imagery
and how we use it. Imagery does not turn God into
anything, it is given to us to try out, to see how it
illuminates our understanding. It can sometimes lead us
to further exploration. Julian let the 'God as mother'
imagery lead her on to thinking afresh about God's
dealings with us:

> The mother can give her child to suck of her
> milk, but our precious Mother Jesus can feed
> us with himself, and does, most courteously
> and tenderly, with the blessed sacrament,
> which is the precious food of true life; and
> with all the sweet sacraments he sustains us
> most mercifully and graciously, and so he
> meant in these blessed words where he said: I
> am he whom Holy Church preaches and

> teaches to you. That is to say: all the health
> and life of the sacraments, all the power and
> grace of my word, all the goodness which is
> ordained in Holy Church for you, I am he.

and

> This fair lovely word 'mother' is so sweet and
> so kind in itself that it cannot truly be said of
> anyone or to anyone except of him and to him
> who is the true Mother of life and of all things.
> To the property of motherhood belong nature,
> love, wisdom and knowledge, and this is God.
> For though it may be so that our bodily
> bringing to birth is only little, humble and
> simple in comparison with our spiritual
> bringing to birth, still it is he who does it in
> the creatures by whom it is done. The kind,
> loving mother who knows and sees the need of
> her child guards it very tenderly, as the nature
> and condition of motherhood will have. And
> always as the child grows in age and in
> stature, she acts differently, but she does not
> change her love.
> (LT Ch 60)

Julian didn't try to pin God down in her use of the
'mother' image – she plays with it, sometimes calling
Jesus our mother, even though of all the ways in which we
encounter God, Jesus is a masculine manifestation of God.

Imagery changes. Sometimes it serves its purpose and
dies out. It is also worth noting that imagery can be killed
by experience. One student I knew couldn't bear to come
to Morning Prayer at the chaplaincy in the university
where I worked for a time, on the day that Anselm's
canticle was used. She called it the chicken song, and said
that she couldn't bear to think of God as a battery hen. She
had no experience of free-range hens, and it was useless to
describe to her how hens brood their young: the picture in

her head was different. Father/Mother can be equally difficult for some people to take. Even though we all probably have an idea of what a father/mother should be – even if only at the level of 'I wish my father/mother was more like yours' – our actual experience of our parents colours the way the imagery works for us.

Sometimes, too, imagery can turn into idolatry if we are not careful. God is always greater than our imagination can suggest, and if we refuse to explore imagery and limit ourselves to certain categories of language, we may find ourselves always in want, as Julian would say. If, with her, we pray that God would, of his goodness, give us himself, we have to be willing to let God surprise us into fresh understanding.

The English language is very rich, but it is also restricting in that its personal pronouns are all gender-specific (except 'it' which doesn't seem an appropriate pronoun to use in respect of God). Middle Eastern languages don't have these pronouns – in the Arabic-speaking world, God is God. Using 'she' instead of 'he' is not particularly helpful – we need words and images that go beyond gender. We have to work quite hard not to be gender-specific, but it can be done. Julian's words can encourage us to be more adventurous in the language and imagery we employ when we think or talk about God.

Questions to consider

1. What imagery do you find helpful in relating to God? What is unhelpful?

2. What does Julian's imagery of God as mother add to your understanding of God?

3. What new imagery have you discovered for yourself that you would like to share with others?

4. How do you react to gender-specific language in prayers and hymns? Is there anything in the liturgy

used in your church which you think could helpfully be changed?

Suggestion for worship at the end of the session

Settle to stillness, using music or a hymn

Our Father, God almighty, is full of strength and goodness, in him we have our being:
We come to God our Father with confidence, for our fragmented lives to be knit together again.
As truly as God is our Father, so is also God our Mother, full of wisdom, tenderness and love:
To God our Mother we come with confidence, to be restored in love.
God is also the Holy Spirit, active in us through grace, praying through us and enabling us to yield ourselves to God:
To God the Holy Spirit we come with confidence, to be opened to God's grace.
God the Trinity is strength and goodness, Wisdom, tenderness and love, who never leaves us:
God, of your goodness, give us yourself, for if we ask anything which is less we shall always be in want. Only in you we have all.

Time for reflection on some words from Mother Julian

Therefore it is our part to love our God in whom we have our being, reverently thanking him for our creation, mightily praying to our Mother for mercy and pity, and to the Lord the Holy Spirit for help and grace. (LT Ch 59)

Prayer for the world and for ourselves. (Anselm's canticle)

> *Gather your little ones to you, o God,*
> *as a hen gathers her brood to protect them.*

> Jesus, as a mother you gather your people to you,
> you are gentle with us as a mother with her children.

> Often you weep over our sins and our pride,
> tenderly you draw us from hatred and judgement.

> You comfort us in sorrow and bind up our wounds,
> in sickness you nurse us and with pure milk you feed
> us.

> Jesus, by your dying we are born to new life,
> by your anguish and labour we come forth in joy.

> Despair turns to hope through your great goodness,
> through your gentleness we find comfort in fear.

> Your warmth gives life to the dead,
> your touch makes sinners righteous.

> Lord Jesus, in your mercy heal us,
> in your love and tenderness remake us.

> In your compassion bring grace and forgiveness,
> for the beauty of heaven may your love prepare us.

> *Gather your little ones to you, o God,*
> *as a hen gathers her brood to protect them.*

Blessing

God's great goodness fills all his creatures
and all his blessed works full,
and endlessly overflows in them;
for he is everlastingness,
and he made us only for himself,
and restored us by his precious Passion.
May he always preserve us in his blessed love,
and all this of his goodness. **Amen.**

We go in the peace of Christ. **Amen.**

3

Prayer

When Jesus was asked by his disciples for some help with prayer, he set his answer in the context of relationship: 'Say "Father" ' (Luke 11.2). Whatever imagery we find helpful (see Chapter 2), prayer is still about our relationship with God. Prayer is the lifeblood of our relationship with this father/mother God, the means by which we and God give to and receive from each other. Prayer comes from God and makes us like God; and, as we saw in the first chapter, God's love is so great that he regards us as partners in his work when we pray. But that work of intercession is only part of prayer. As with any relationship, joint action springs out of knowledge and love.

Julian said that God delights in our prayer even when we feel that we are not getting anywhere, for the act of coming to God in prayer is a sign of our desire. And the end of all our prayer is to know God:

> Our good Lord revealed that it is very greatly pleasing to him that a simple soul should come naked, openly and familiarly. For this is the loving yearning of the soul through the touch of the Holy Spirit, from the understanding which I have in this revelation: God, of your goodness give me yourself, for you are enough for me, and I can ask for nothing which is less which can pay you full worship. And if I ask anything which is less, always I am in want; but only in you do I have everything.
> (LT Ch 5)

As a child I was taught to say my prayers. It was one of the things that gave me a framework for growth, like learning to wash and clean my teeth; eat a balanced diet; get adequate rest. It was some time before I realized that these requirements were not ends in themselves, to be done and forgotten about until the next time, but aids to living a full and balanced life. The intention behind the constant reminders was to get me into the habit of doing the things that were necessary for my health, to enable them to become second nature for me. I began to realize, too, that not all the questions beginning 'Have you ...?' carried the same weight. Like the music practice that I was often reminded about, which was intended to help me become more musical, saying my prayers was meant to help me to become more prayerful. No one actually said that. I was left, on the whole, to find out for myself that 'saying prayers' was only a part of living a prayerful life. The 'prayer time' was really the 'practice time', and the effort of practice would bear fruit in what happened as a result in the rest of my life. Archbishop William Temple put it helpfully when he said that although most people think that behaviour matters and prayer helps it, the truth is that prayer matters, and behaviour tests it.[1]

When we consider prayer in the context of a relationship, we can perhaps begin to see that prayer has to be far more than asking, though that is probably where we began. Indeed, Jesus' teaching about prayer contains quite a lot about asking. But we learn fairly early on in our childhood that making demands comes second in importance to acknowledging relationships. The first words most people learn are 'Thank you'. 'Please' comes next. It is not often that we would ask total strangers for what we want – giving and receiving depend on there being a prior relationship. Jesus' teaching about asking in prayer was set in the context of a life lived in awareness of the Father's presence and he was talking to people of faith whose lives were rooted in the concept of being God's chosen people.

We spend a great deal of time building up relationships in the course of our life. Their depth depends on the amount of attention that we give to them. The difficulty in building up a relationship with God is that God isn't visibly present to relate to. Relationships grow when we spend what we call 'quality time' with each other. But they don't stop when we cease to be present to the people with whom we are in relationship. We don't stop being a son or daughter or parent or friend just because we are out of sight. But we know that relationships can die if we don't spend time on them. So we need our times when we can give ourselves a chance to be loved by God, and learn to love God in return.

One of the greatest enemies to enabling relationships to grow is our preoccupation with being busy. The protestant work ethic has a lot to answer for! It isn't only our culture that defines who we are by what we do, the Church has a propensity for keeping us occupied too. The sentiments behind hymns such as 'Father, hear the prayer we offer', with its insistence that we need to keep at it, spiritually, need to be challenged:

The prayer we offer
Not for ease? Why not?
What's wrong with ease?
For most of us the
Problem is not self-indulgence,
But that we allow ourselves too little.
Prohibitions, counsels of perfection,
Drive us and load us up with guilt.

Time enough for courageous living
And all that rock-smiting.
Let's rest and wander in green pastures
When we find them, make the space
To let ourselves be loved;
Build up our strength
And grow in confidence;
Drink living water springing in

Great fountains;
Feed on the Bread of Life which
Satisfies.

Then we shall have provision
For the journey, and at last
Arrive, not too unpractised
In the art of resting
In his presence.[2]

Julian said that our prayer delights God:

Our Lord is most glad and joyful because of
our prayer; and he expects it and he wants to
have it, for with his grace it makes us like to
himself in condition as we are in nature, and
such is his blessed will.
(LT Ch 41)

But Julian recognized that prayer isn't always a delight
for us, and what she goes on to say demonstrates that she
knew from experience that there are times when prayer
goes dead, when there seems little point to it, when we
don't seem to be getting anywhere. It isn't only when
prayer seems to be unanswered that it is hard going.
Julian continues,

For he says: Pray wholeheartedly, though it
seems that this has no savour for you; still it is
profitable enough, though you may not feel
that. Pray wholeheartedly, though you may
feel nothing, though you may see nothing, yes,
though you think that you could not, for in
dryness and in barrenness, in sickness and in
weakness, then is your prayer most pleasing
to me, though you think it almost tasteless to
you.
(LT Ch 41)

Julian knew about the difficulties from experience,
then. But she would probably also have had recourse to
advice about coping with the difficulty of dealing with that

kind of weariness in prayer. The Rule Aelred of Rievaulx wrote for his sister suggested that it is sometimes more profitable to pray for shorter periods than for long stretches at a time, except when she found herself caught up in God's love. He also suggested that it might be a good idea to vary the ways in which she prayed, using Psalms when they kept her attention, changing over to reading when the Psalms palled, going back to saying prayers when the reading became difficult to sustain. When all else failed, he said, engage in some manual work.[3] That is advice which has stood the test of time.

We cannot expect our spiritual life, any more than any other aspect of life, to be lived on the heights. We have our high moments, but we can't prolong them: as soon as we try to clutch hold of them, they are gone. Most of our lives are lived out in the humdrum business of everyday relationships. We can relate to the experience of Peter, James and John at the Transfiguration: they were caught up into a great spiritual experience, and Peter would have loved to have stayed there for ever. But even as he said so, the vision faded, and they had to go back to living life at the bottom of the mountain, with all its difficulties as well as its opportunities (Luke 9.18–43). The test of our commitment to relationships lies in how we continue in the business of daily life. Faithfulness in prayer is part of our commitment to our relationship with God.

Prayer is essential to our life with God. But there are difficulties that get in the way of the 'practice time' which prevent prayer from becoming our way of life. For example, most of us live busy lives – there isn't time to fit everything in, let alone take time out for prayer. But it is surprising what we do find we have time for if we really want to do it. If prayer really is the lifeblood of our relationship with God, it needs to be given high priority. If we can begin to establish this relationship when life is fairly straightforward, when we feel more or less in control of our time, then when circumstances make it impossible to give as much time as we would like, we have a reservoir of experience to draw on. Parents with small children, for example, or anyone who cares for another on a full-time basis, are unlikely to find much time for peace and quiet. Then we have to take opportunities when they arise, recalling the presence of God which we learned to value when circumstances were easier. Prayer means putting ourselves where God can catch our attention, and love us into wholeness.

Another of the difficulties that people often identify about prayer is that when we do try to settle down, we find that our thoughts go off in all directions. That is not really surprising, because we are usually juggling with all that we have on our minds in the course of our daily life. We don't suddenly change just because we have decided to spend time in prayer. We really don't have to beat ourselves up about being creatures with a short attention span. When we do find our thoughts straying, we need to bring them back gently to what we really want to attend to. One helpful way to get focused is to replace all the other things we have on our minds with a rhythm prayer (sometimes called a mantra) which we can use to bring ourselves back when our thoughts wander off. It might be a short text from Scripture: 'My heart longs for you' (Psalm 42) or 'My Lord and my God' (John 20.28); or 'Only in you I have all' (Mother Julian).

It may be that it seems as though most of our prayer time has been spent in bringing ourselves back to God. Many people experience that. Archbishop Michael Ramsey was once asked by a reporter if he had said his prayers that morning. The Archbishop replied that he had. Not recognizing a good stopping place when she met one, the reporter continued, 'How long did you spend on your prayers?' 'About a minute,' the Archbishop replied. 'But it took me twenty-nine minutes to get there.' We can take heart from his experience. Gradually we learn inner stillness, and we can carry that with us and practise it in our daily life, not just in 'prayer time'.

Another hindrance to perseverance is the feeling that our prayer isn't heard because it isn't answered – at least we don't notice any difference. Julian had some words of encouragement for those occasions too:

> Sometimes it comes to our mind that we have prayed a long time, and it still seems to us that we do not have what we ask for. But we should not be too depressed on this account, for I am sure, according to our Lord's meaning, that either we are waiting for a better occasion, or for more grace, or a better gift.
> (LT Ch 42)

Julian believed that God loves us and delights in us, and wants us to love him and delight in him. That is at the heart of our relationship with God, and it's at the heart of this way of praying too. Julian didn't write anything about 'methods' of praying. She did note that there were some essential elements in our exercise of prayer, but she did not divide them into separate categories. For her, the experience of forgiveness led naturally to expressions of love and thankfulness, and deeper longing for God; and these flowed naturally out of and into each other. She described the daily round of prayer times, and spoke quite naturally about these times of prayer leading into contemplating God's love. She didn't draw distinctions between that contemplation and going about her daily business – it was all the context of God's love for her, and hers for God.

Much has been written about methods of prayer, and if we are not careful they can become ends in themselves. It used to be the case that anyone asking for advice about prayer would be presented with a programme which led from what was called 'Vocal prayer' (saying prayers), through various stages of 'Meditation' (thinking about God as revealed in Scripture), to 'Affective prayer' (expressing desire for God). Beyond this, for really holy people lay the heights of 'Contemplation'. Many people over the years have struggled with a 'method' which got them nowhere, when recognition of their natural inclinations and temperament would have led them to grow spiritually without quite so much frustration. Contemplation is not a goal to aim at, but a gift, as all prayer is, from God, and we don't have to reach a certain standard of holiness, whatever that might mean, before we can be caught up in it.

What we call Contemplative Prayer is not a specialist activity undertaken by people who are particularly holy, it is very simple. Indeed, it is sometimes called 'The Prayer of Simplicity', or 'The Prayer of Simple Regard'. It corresponds to the stage in a relationship when we don't need to talk, but can simply be with another person enjoying their company, and letting them enjoy being with us. There is a well-known story about a French peasant who used to go into his local church every day, and spend some time there. When he was asked what he did during that time, he said in some surprise, 'I don't do anything. I just look at God, and God looks at me.' Reaching this stage of awareness may take years, or it may come very early on. Small children have a natural gift for being caught up in wonder – and Jesus said we need to be like children. It is a gift – we can't make it happen, but we can dispose ourselves to receive it. We all know that at times we get caught up in something, and don't know where the time has gone. Practical skills in art, music and dance can bring us to the same kind of stillness, as well as the activities we more readily call prayer. The stillness is always God's gift. We never achieve great heights of devotion by our own efforts – it is always God who prays in us. Lovely though it would be always to feel God's presence with us when we come to prayer, that sense of presence is not ours to command. Prayer is always God's work in us, God's gift to us, and our part is to be faithful, open to God's coming. It is our being prepared that matters.

Having this prayerful attitude to life does not mean that we are good at prayer – to paraphrase Julian, we are not good because we pray in this way, we are only good if we love God better.

For just over 30 years, groups of people from all Christian denominations have been gathering to wait on God in this way. Often called Julian Groups, they draw their inspiration from the example of Julian, and practise waiting on God in stillness. Many people find that there is support in the company of others, and the experience of meeting together encourages them to continue to pray in this way in the times between meetings.[4]

Questions to consider

1. How has your prayer changed in the course of your life? Do you feel that it would be helpful to have some more guidance?

2. What have you found helpful in learning to still your mind when you come to your prayer time?

3. Would it be helpful to have more periods of quiet in times of public worship? If so, where would you like to place them?

4. Would it be appropriate to think about setting up a Julian Group in your area?

Notes

1. After William Temple: 'The proper relation in thought between prayer and conduct is not that conduct is supremely important and prayer may help it, but that prayer is supremely important and conduct tests it.' From *Christus Veritas*, published Macmillan 1924. Quoted by Gordon Mursell in *English Spirituality: Vol. 2, From 1700 to the Present Day, p. 373*, SPCK.

2. 'The prayer we offer', from *Watching for the Kingfisher*, Canterbury Press 2009.

3. *The Works of Aelred of Rievaulx*, A Rule of Life for a Recluse, Part 1, The outer man, p. 55.

4. See information about Julian Meetings on p. 62.

Suggestion for worship at the end of the session

Settle to stillness, using music or a hymn

Our Father, God almighty, is full of strength and goodness, in him we have our being:
We come to God our Father with confidence, for our fragmented lives to be knit together again.
As truly as God is our Father, so is also God our Mother, full of wisdom, tenderness and love:
To God our Mother we come with confidence, to be restored in love.
God is also the Holy Spirit, active in us through grace, praying through us and enabling us to yield ourselves to God:
To God the Holy Spirit we come with confidence, to be opened to God's grace.
God the Trinity is strength and goodness, Wisdom, tenderness and love, who never leaves us:
God, of your goodness, give us yourself, for if we ask anything which is less we shall always be in want. Only in you we have all.

Time for reflection on some words from Mother Julian

Pray wholeheartedly, though it seems that this has no savour for you; still it is profitable enough, though you may not feel that. Pray wholeheartedly, though you may feel nothing, though you may see nothing, yes, though you think that you could not, for in dryness and in barrenness, in sickness and in weakness, then is your prayer most pleasing to me, though you think it almost tasteless to you. (LT Ch 41)

Prayer
My God, I desire to love thee
with all my heart
which thou madest for thyself;
with all my mind
which only thou can'st satisfy;
with all my soul
which longs to soar to thee;
with all my strength, my feeble strength,
which shrinks before so great a task,
and yet can choose nought else
but spend itself in loving thee.

Claim thou my heart,
fill thou my mind,
uplift my soul and
reinforce my strength,
that where I fail,
thou mayest succeed in me,
and make me love thee perfectly.

W. H. Frere

Blessing
God's great goodness fills all his creatures
and all his blessed works full,
and endlessly overflows in them;
for he is everlastingness,
and he made us only for himself,
and restored us by his precious Passion.
May he always preserve us in his blessed love,
and all this of his goodness. **Amen.**

We go in the peace of Christ. **Amen.**

4

Sin

When God wraps us round and enfolds us like our clothing, as Julian put it, he enfolds every part of us in unconditional love. God doesn't just enfold the parts of our nature we would call holy and good, but the parts we don't like very much, and the parts we hope others will never discover. John V. Taylor, in *The Christlike God*, says:

> What God loves is nothing but the whole – the whole self in the whole situation. That and nothing else is what is present to God: *all* present. Making a present to God of one's whole self, that is love for God. Being all present, all *now* that is love for God. This entails calling in one's self from the past, the regrets, and resentments and scars, and presenting them to the eyes of his love. It entails calling in one's self from the future, the day-dreams, the fears, the ambitions, and presenting them, leaving them with him. It entails calling in the self from beyond the pale[1] the self that would properly be banned from one's autobiography but is a true part of the one God loves.

The biblical view of human nature is that we are made in the image of God, made to reflect God's nature. When God saw everything that he had made, it was very good. And if we have ever made anything and said 'Gosh, that's good', we can begin to understand something of God's delight in us.

That's not the whole story, of course. Things went wrong, what we call sin broke in to spoil God's intention, and the image was marred. Julian thought deeply about this, and wondered how the great harm done by sin to God's creatures could be remedied. And the Lord assured her that although Adam's sin was the greatest harm ever done, it is more profitable to concentrate her thoughts on the atonement, for the saving act of God in Christ is much greater than the sin which made atonement necessary.

> Ah, good Lord, how could all things be well, because of the great harm which has come through sin to your creatures? And here I wished, so far as I dared, for some plainer explanation through which I might be at ease in this matter. And to this our blessed Lord answered, very meekly and with a most loving manner, and he showed that Adam's sin was the greatest harm ever done or ever to be done until the end of the world. And he showed me that this is plainly known to all Holy Church upon earth.

> Furthermore, he taught me that I should contemplate the glorious atonement, for this atoning is more pleasing to the blessed divinity and more honourable for man's salvation than ever Adam's sin was harmful.
> (LT Ch 29)

God has dealt with sin, and when we feel that we are not worthy of God's love, when sin puts a barrier between us and God, it is a barrier that comes from our side, not God's. We need to keep our sense of sin in proportion, and not wallow in seventeenth-century language about being miserable sinners. Most of us do not sin deliberately, whatever liturgical prayers would have us say – we are far more likely to fall into sin through carelessness. As I was looking at a crucifix one day, a shaft of light directed my attention to one particular feature of it:

For my salvation
His bloodied knees
Caught my attention ...

I've grown accustomed
To the sight of blood
Pouring from thorn-crowned head
And marks of nails and spear:
The crucified Christ
Bearing the sins of the world.
A distant Christ, carrying
The big sins – murder,
Premeditated cruelty –
Other people's sins, not often mine.
(Although I have it in me.)

But the sore knees
Brought him close.
That blood comes from
Everyone's experience.
Tripped up by inattention,
Undue haste, or thoughtlessness,
We feel the sting.
Those sins I know,
Catching me unaware.

It was the weight of such sins
Caused him to fall under the cross
And graze his knees.

Should I not then cry, Mercy?[2]

Julian had some liberating things to say about sin. It is nothing, she said. Julian was not suggesting that sin doesn't exist:

> It is the sharpest scourge with which any chosen soul can be struck.
> (LT Ch 39)

But sin has no status. Julian saw that although the tendency to sin is part of our human nature, God is never angry with us because of sin:

> It seemed to me that it was necessary to see and to know that we are sinners and commit many evil deeds which we ought to forsake, and leave many good deeds undone which we ought to do, so that we deserve pain, blame and wrath. And despite all this, I saw truly that our Lord was never angry, and never will be. Because he is God, he is good, he is truth, he is love, he is peace; and his power, his wisdom, his charity and his unity do not allow him to be angry.
> (LT Ch 46)

Julian saw that God leads us by his Holy Spirit to desire mercy, and then through contrition, compassion and true longing for God, God restores us to wholeness. This experience of restoration was what Julian herself prayed she would receive by means of the three wounds which she requested in her original prayer. (See Introduction, p. 7).

Julian made extensive use of an allegory in developing her ideas about sin and forgiveness. There was a lord who had a servant who stood in attendance, ready to do his master's will. When the lord sent the servant to perform a task, the servant rushed off at great speed, tripped and fell into a ditch. He was in great distress, not only because he was hurt, but also because face down in the ditch, he could not see his master. The lord, meanwhile looked on with compassion because he saw that it was the servant's eagerness to do his will which had caused him to stumble. He did not blame the servant for falling, indeed, so great was his pity for him that he wished to reward him for his service. (See LT Chs 51–52)

Since we have been restored by God's mercy and grace, God does not want us to let consciousness of sin stand between us and God, because nothing will stop God loving us:

> Our courteous Lord does not want his servants to despair because they fall often and grievously; for our falling does not hinder him in loving us.
> (LT Ch 39)

Julian has a very matter of fact approach to sin —we sin because it is in our nature to do so, and God loves us endlessly, and God is always gentle with us in the way that he makes us aware of our sin. For Julian, feelings of guilt and worthlessness are far more damaging than the failures we call sin, for guilt and a sense of worthlessness fix our attention on ourselves. Julian says that the important thing is that we are forgiven:

> For we do not fall in the sight of God, and we do not stand in our own sight; and both of these are true, as I see it, but the contemplating of our Lord God is the higher truth. So we are much indebted to him, that he will in this way of life reveal to us this high truth, and I understand that while we are in this way it is most profitable to us that we see these both together. For the higher contemplation keeps us in spiritual joy and true delight in God; the other, which is the lower contemplation, keeps us in fear, and makes us ashamed of ourselves. (LT Ch 82)

This approach is most liberating, but the Church has not always adopted it. Augustine, in the fourth century, maintained that we are all essentially tainted with sin, and persuaded the Church to condemn as a heretic Pelagius who maintained that people are essentially good because at their heart they bear the image of God. Ever since, the Church has been rather better at reminding people that

they are sinners than at encouraging them to rejoice in
God's forgiveness.

John V. Taylor in *The Christlike God* makes this point
when he writes:

> How regrettable it is, how unnatural in fact,
> that through the centuries the confessional
> stalls round the walls of many churches have
> received the secrets of so many sins, and have
> not been equally available for the confidences
> of men and women who have been overtaken
> by the ecstasies or insights or consolations
> that declare the reality of God! Had this other
> side of personal experience been invited, no
> doubt there would have been the same
> amount of fantasy, neurosis and self-
> advertisement as has always been exhibited in
> the confessional, and wise priests would have
> known how to discern and guide as they
> have done hitherto. No doubt they would have
> found the recitals of glory just as repetitive as
> the catalogues of sin, for the accounts of these
> intensely private memories are uncannily
> similar. But at least it might have redressed
> the balance and made the churches
> everywhere as mindful of divine initiative as
> of human failure.[3]

Of course we have to remember that we are sinners, but
we don't have to be obsessed by that memory – the higher
contemplation of God's forgiveness is what we are called
to. Perhaps we are reluctant to accept that we are forgiven,
because we confuse thinking of ourselves as forgiven with
fear of giving the impression that we think we are already
perfect. A wayside pulpit I passed recently proclaimed,
'Christians are not perfect, they are just forgiven.' That is
the distinction we need to bear in mind. Knowing
ourselves to be forgiven leads not to pride, but to deep
thankfulness. Fear of pride can lead us to the kind of false

humility which keeps our attention firmly fixed on ourselves. It can lead us to go on insisting that we are not worthy to be loved by God, as though we have somehow to persuade God to do what God already does because that is his nature.

It is helpful to think about Paul making his claim that all he cares about is to know Christ, and following it with the disclaimer 'not that I have already obtained this ... but I press on to make it my own, because Christ Jesus has made me his own' (Philippians 3.10-12). We are precious and honoured and loved, as Isaiah said (Isaiah 43.4); 'God's work of art', as Paul said (Ephesians 2.12, Jerusalem Bible translation). But we are not there yet – we are on-the-way people, like the figures Michelangelo left partly released from their marble blocks.[4] But Julian's insight was that God sees our potential, and continually releases us from all that holds us back from loving him.

To begin to believe that would be to begin to take the idea of God as Father/Mother seriously. Parents when asked about their children do not normally begin with a catalogue of their faults, they talk about them with pride in their development and achievements. When they do talk about their faults, they often do so with a wry smile.

Perhaps that's how God regards our faults sometimes. For God is always more interested in our growth in love, and is quicker than we are to see our failures as part of that growth, as Julian suggested in her allegory.

Questions for consideration

1. Do Julian's words, 'We do not fall in the sight of God, and we do not stand in our own sight', help us to understand what penitence is about?

2. Do the liturgies of our churches help us to get sin and forgiveness in perspective?

3. Are there any changes you would like to see in liturgical practice in your own church?

Notes

1. J. V. Taylor, *The Christlike God*, SCM Press 1992, p. 278.

2. Ann Lewin, 'For my Salvation' in *Watching for the Kingfisher*, Canterbury Press 2009.

3. J. V. Taylor, *The Christlike God*, SCM Press 1992, p. 55.

4. Michelangelo: *The bearded slave* and *The awakening slave* in Florence, Accademia di Belle Arte.

5. George Herbert, 'Love'.

Suggestion for worship at the end of the session

Settle to stillness, using music or a hymn

Our Father, God almighty, is full of strength and goodness, in him we have our being:
We come to God our Father with confidence, for our fragmented lives to be knit together again.
As truly as God is our Father, so is also God our Mother, full of wisdom, tenderness and love:
To God our Mother we come with confidence, to be restored in love.
God is also the Holy Spirit, active in us through grace, praying through us and enabling us to yield ourselves to God:
To God the Holy Spirit we come with confidence, to be opened to God's grace.
God the Trinity is strength and goodness, Wisdom, tenderness and love, who never leaves us:
God, of your goodness, give us yourself, for if we ask anything which is less we shall always be in want. Only in you we have all.

Time for reflection on some words from Mother Julian

We do not fall in the sight of God, and we do not stand in our own sight; and both of these are true, as I see it, but the contemplating of our Lord God is the higher truth. So we are much indebted to him, that he will in this way of life reveal to us this high truth, and I understand that while we are in this way it is most profitable to us that we see these both together. For the higher contemplation keeps us in spiritual joy and true delight in God; the other, which is the lower contemplation, keeps us in fear, and makes us ashamed of ourselves. (LT Ch 82)

Pray for the world and for ourselves, that we may all come to understand the amazing generosity of God's love.

Love bade me welcome: yet my soul drew back,
    Guilty of dust and sin.
But quick-eyed Love, observing me grow slack
    From my first entrance in,
Drew nearer to me, sweetly questioning
    If I lacked anything.

A guest, I answered, worthy to be here:
    Love said, You shall be he.
I the unkind, ungrateful? Ah, my dear,
    I cannot look on thee.
Love took my hand, and smiling did reply
    Who made the eyes but I?

Truth, Lord, but I have marred them: let my shame
    Go where it doth deserve.
And know you not, says Love, who bore the blame?
    My dear, then I will serve.
You must sit down, says Love, and taste my meat.
    So I did sit and eat.

George Herbert[5]

Blessing

God's great goodness fills all his creatures
and all his blessed works full,
and endlessly overflows in them;
for he is everlastingness,
and he made us only for himself,
and restored us by his precious Passion.
May he always preserve us in his blessed love,
and all this of his goodness. **Amen.**

We go in the peace of Christ. **Amen.**

5

All Shall Be Well

'All shall be well' is one of Julian's best-known sayings, but we could be forgiven, perhaps, for responding, 'You must be joking.' How can anyone who is aware of the reality of life say that all will be well? Christians are sometimes guilty of offering the kind of facile comfort that says, 'Don't worry, things will be better tomorrow.' Experience tells us that they may very well be worse. Julian lived at a time when there were many challenges to well-being, and she must have said 'All shall be well' through gritted teeth sometimes: she knew, as we do, that it is a struggle to hold on to that belief when there is so much around us to challenge it.

Quite near to the beginning of her reflections, Julian records her vision of the little thing no bigger than a hazel nut, which she fears will disintegrate because it is so small. She is assured that it and everything else in creation exists because God loves it, and God's love will protect and sustain all he has made. That did not stop Julian questioning God:

> It seemed to me impossible that every kind of thing should be well, and to this I had no answer from our Lord except this, what is impossible to you is not impossible to me. I shall preserve my word in everything, and I shall make everything well.
> (LT Ch 32)

It is that truth that we need to hang on to when faced with suffering. Whatever happens, we are loved by God.

The fact of suffering is probably the biggest challenge to faith that we encounter. We cry out in anguish, 'Why does God allow it? What have I/we/they done to deserve it?'

People sometimes say that suffering is sent to test us. It is difficult to square that with the God revealed in Jesus who made it plain that suffering is not what God wants. Jesus healed the sick, and challenged people who oppressed others. 'I came that they may have life, and have it abundantly,' he said (John 10.10).

Nor is it easy to square what we know of God with the idea that somehow we deserve what we get. The answer to the question 'What have I done to deserve this?' is, usually, 'Nothing.' Of course there is suffering we bring on ourselves. But it is the consequence of our folly, of choices that we make about our lifestyle. We can't say that it is a punishment. Some suffering is undoubtedly caused by sin, but it is not the sin of those who suffer which brings it about, but the sin of those who hold life cheap. And some suffering is caused because the natural world behaves in the way the natural world behaves. No one could say that the suffering experienced by those caught up in the tsunami on Boxing Day 2004, or the earthquake in Pakistan in 2006, was because of their sin. Jesus met the same question head-on when he was told about the suffering of some Galileans who had been slaughtered by Roman authority. He asked his informers: 'Do you think that because these Galileans suffered in this way they were worse sinners than all other Galileans? ... Or those eighteen who were killed when the tower of Siloam fell on them – do you think that they were worse offenders than all the others living in Jerusalem?' (Luke 13.1–4). Jesus didn't give any answer to his question – but he did take the opportunity to remind his hearers of the need for repentance. Turning our lives round so that we live more in accord with God's will is always a good response to tragedy.

The question 'Why does God allow suffering?' probably brings us to the heart of our problem. If God is all-powerful, and the experience of suffering is not part of his intention for humanity, why doesn't God put an end to it?

If he could put an end to it, but chooses not to, is he a God worth worshipping?

Part of our difficulty lies with the vocabulary we use in talking about God. For many people, words like 'almighty', 'powerful', come to our lips very easily. And as we were thinking before in Chapter 2, much of our concept of God seems to have been derived from the Old Testament view of a God who was often unpredictable, and who did act in retribution against those who opposed his will. The idea of a God who is out to get us seems to have a scriptural basis. But that is only the case if we discount the idea that people's concept of God grew as they sought to understand him, and opened themselves up to his revelation of his nature. The God we see in Jesus is a God who made himself vulnerable. This was not the first time God had put himself at the mercy of his creation: when he gave humans responsibility, which is another way of describing free will, he took a risk. And in the incarnation the vulnerability was made even more obvious, as God in Jesus was brought to his knees, suffered with us, and loved humanity through the pain of rejection and crucifixion. We can never say to God, 'You don't know what it's like.' The cross shows us that God does know. And the resurrection of Jesus shows us that the God who knows what it is like to suffer seeks continually to bring new life out of dead ends.

Whatever imagery we use for God has to take account of God's vulnerability, and the vulnerability of love that will go to any lengths to give us life and wholeness. Suffering is part of how the world is, and God's faithful love is part of how the world is, too.

Vulnerable
We've been here before, Lord,
You and I. A situation
Not of your will, and
Certainly not my choice.

I can't believe that you send
Suffering, and I don't want it.
We look at each other,
And feel the pain
That this is how it is.

I do not acquiesce
Without complaint;
And yet the words die on my lips,
For in response you come
With wounded hands
And cradle me in love.[1]

But where does prayer fit into our struggle to make sense of our world? We have thought already, in Chapter 1, about the problem of apparently unanswered prayer when we were considering the nature of intercession. Is there anything we can add now?

Perhaps we could look again at what we think we are doing when we pray for people who are in need of any kind. Probably most of our prayer in this area concerns people who are ill. Our natural desire is that they should get better. But that may, humanly speaking, be impossible. I was faced with this quite sharply when my father was diagnosed with cancer. I desperately wanted him to get better, and that is what I prayed for: that he would be cured. But the skill of the surgeons couldn't eliminate the cancer, and it became obvious that his condition was terminal. As his illness progressed, and death came nearer, my prayer changed. I found myself praying that he would be healed. And that prayer included the certainty that he would die. Healing and cure are not the same. My father was not cured, but I'm sure that there was healing, and not just for him. It was reflected in the way we related to him as a family, in the way he faced his pain with courage and dignity, in the way that we were able to accept his death as the ultimate act of healing for him. Healing doesn't necessarily eliminate pain, but it does move us on.

Healing
What if pain does not go,
What then? Scars can be
Touched to raw response in
Unexpected moments
Long after the event which
Caused them, nerve ends twitch
Perhaps for ever after
Amputation.

Healing is not achieved
Without some cost. It
May not mean the end of
Pain. Healing can hurt
Just like fresh wounds,
As pockets of poison are
Lanced, or lesions cut to
Allow more flexibility. For
Healing is not going back
To what one was before,
It is a growing on
To a new stage of being,
Through many deaths and
Resurrections being set free.[2]

Prayer changed, for me, in that experience. And I began to think that perhaps we don't have to be too specific in our requests. A useful model for intercession can be the account of the four men who brought their friend to Jesus, in the event recorded in Mark 2.1–12. We often miss the fact that they simply brought the man. They didn't ask for anything at all. If they had asked for something, it might well have been that their friend would be able to walk again. That was obviously what was wrong with him. And if they had asked that, no doubt Jesus would have restored the man's mobility. But perhaps the man would have walked away still carrying the problem that was much more deep-seated than physical paralysis. Jesus went to the heart of the problem and told him that he was forgiven. Whatever it was that was paralysing him did not stop God loving him, and there was no reason to go on as though he hadn't got a leg to stand on. I don't think Jesus was saying that the man's paralysis was the result of sin – but he was pointing out that illness isn't always what it appears to be. We understand more of psychosomatic manifestations now than Jesus' contemporaries did.

Perhaps one of the reasons why prayer sometimes seems to be unanswered is that we have simply been asking for the wrong things. Our prayer may initially be more about what we want than about what God wants. When we overhear Jesus praying in Gethsemane, perhaps that is what we hear: the thought of suffering is overwhelming, and his natural reaction is to shrink from it. But when he goes on to say, 'Yet not my will but yours be done' (Luke 22.42) he is not suggesting that the suffering is God's will. He is saying, 'If the only way that evil can be overcome by love is by my refusing to hit back at those who will kill me, then I will embrace what comes.' It is a prayer of trust that his sacrifice will not be wasted, that all will in the end be well.

Jesus couldn't be spared suffering, neither will we avoid it. Suffering is part of the world as it is. But because of what Jesus accomplished on the cross, it is not the last word. God has the last word, when Jesus says, 'It is finished' (John 19.30).

We won't be spared suffering, but Julian says that the way to meet it is with trust.

> God did not say, You will not be assailed, you will not be belaboured, you will not be disquieted, but he said You will not be overcome. God wants us to pay attention to these words and always be strong in faithful trust in wellbeing and in woe, for he loves us and delights in us, and so he wishes us to love

him and delight in him and trust greatly in
him, and all will be well.
(ST Ch 22)

Dark moments
'All shall be well ...'
She must have said that
Sometimes through gritted teeth.
Surely she knew the moments
When fear gnaws at trust,
The future loses shape,
Gethsemane.

The courage that says
All shall be well
Doesn't mean feeling no fear,
But facing it, trusting
God won't let go.

All shall be well
Doesn't deny present experience
But roots it deep
In the faithfulness of God,
Whose will and gift is life.[3]

If God's will is that we should have life, what do we
make of death? Julian went so far as to pray for an
experience which would help her to understand death.
Most of us shy away from even talking about it. But the
Christian faith has insights which the world is in desperate
need of hearing, hard though it may be to overcome our
inhibitions about broaching the subject.

Ad Quem

Death – terminus,
Heart-stopping jolt
At the end of the line?
Or junction, where worlds meet,
Faith catching the connection?[4]

The one certain thing about us is that we will die. But we don't talk about death unless we have to. In our society we are cushioned from its reality. In spite of the number of violent deaths we see on our TV screens, many people have never seen or touched a dead person; and we keep being assured that steps are being taken to cut down the number of deaths from particular diseases, as though that will mean that some of us won't die at all.

It is good to work at eliminating pain and suffering, and it is natural to feel outrage at premature or violent death. But we seem to have great difficulty in accepting that death is a natural part of life. We have moved a long way from awareness of the natural rhythms of nature. Every year, the seasons remind us of new life growing to maturity and then moving towards death. Observation of the life of trees and plants teaches us that in order for life to continue, it has to progress from one stage to the next. A flower has to die before seed can be set. The seeds have to fall from the plant, apparently dead, before the next cycle of life can begin.

When I was a small child, I used to be puzzled when we prayed in church for people who were dangerously ill. In danger of what, I wondered. Presumably they were in danger of dying. But I also heard in church that there was something called eternal life, which seemed to be on the other side of death. Many years and experiences have intervened, and I've realized that things aren't that simple. Apart from the suffering that sometimes precedes death, there is always pain at the loss of people we love, and there are questions about what happens to us when we die.

Canon Henry Scott Holland, in a sermon preached at the Lying-in-State of Edward VII in 1910, said that we hover between two ways of regarding death. One is that death is the end. We recoil from this death, and protest at it, for it is unbearable to think that we shall never be able to talk to our loved ones, or touch them, again. Death is an insuperable barrier. The other view is that death is nothing at all. The person we loved is no longer there in the coffin in front of us, but they still exist. We go on thinking about them, praying for them, remembering them. This passage from the sermon is often read at funerals. It begins with the words, 'Death is nothing at all'. But taken out of context, the passage is a denial of the reality we are experiencing when we are bereaved. Scott Holland went on to say that we may try to deny the fact of death, because it is so painful. But the feeling of unreality we sometimes have as we look at a dead body and realize that the person we loved is no longer there, will give way to the realization that, far from being nothing at all, death is a hard reality which has made a difference. Our task, he said, is to reconcile both views of death: it is an end, but there is a continuity of growth in the love of God which enables this end to be a new beginning. The sermon was preached at Pentecost, and the preacher reminded his hearers that the gift of the Spirit was the gift of God's life experienced now, so that eternal life is not only life beyond the grave, but a life we begin to live here and now.[5]

When we begin to grasp that idea, we have a new insight to offer. Death is not the worst thing that can happen to us. It is, rather, a natural stage in our growth. In the imagery of the poem 'Ad Quem' above, death is not a terminus, but a junction where worlds meet.

It is faith that catches the connection – and faith is not the same as certainty. Faith is an attitude of trust in the God who is always faithful. We learn that trust through many experiences of letting go in order that new life may grow. There are many deaths and resurrections on the way to fullness of life.

We don't know when we shall die – but we can prepare for it. 'From *sudden* death, Good Lord, deliver us' is a prayer (from the *Book of Common Prayer*), that we will be spared an *unprepared* death. There are, of course, practical things we can do to prepare for death, like making a will, and keeping our affairs in order so that our executors don't have too hard a task. But the deeper preparation lies in attending to our relationship with God, practising God's presence in our lives, making full use of the gift of life which is ours now, and will grow into its fullness in God's love.

Some questions for discussion

1. What are the challenges that face us in learning to trust?

2. What does it mean to you to describe God as 'vulnerable'?

3. What has been your own experience of praying for people who are suffering in some way? How do you respond to the suggestion that we don't need to be too specific in our prayer requests?

4. In what ways do you think that the Church could better help its members, as well as people outside it, to face up to death? Have you thought about your own death? What personal preparations have you made – such as making a will, talking about your funeral?

Notes

1. 'Vulnerable' from *Watching for the Kingfisher*, Canterbury Press 2009.

2. 'Healing' from *Watching for the Kingfisher*.

3. 'Dark Moments' from *Watching for the Kingfisher*.

4. 'Ad Quem' from *Watching for the Kingfisher*.

5. Henry Scott Holland, a sermon published posthumously in *Facts of the Faith*, Longmans 1919.

Suggestion for worship at the end of the session

Settle to stillness, using music or a hymn

Our Father, God almighty, is full of strength and goodness,
in him we have our being:
We come to God our Father with confidence,
for our fragmented lives to be knit together again.
As truly as God is our Father, so is also God our Mother,
full of wisdom, tenderness and love:
To God our Mother we come with confidence,
to be restored in love.
God is also the Holy Spirit, active in us through grace,
praying through us and enabling us to yield ourselves to
God:
To God the Holy Spirit we come with confidence,
to be opened to God's grace.
God the Trinity is strength and goodness,
Wisdom, tenderness and love, who never leaves us:
God, of your goodness, give us yourself,
for if we ask anything which is less
we shall always be in want.
Only in you we have all.

Time for reflection on some words from Mother Julian

God did not say, You will not be troubled, you will not be
belaboured, you will not be disquieted, but he said, You
will not be overcome. God wants us to pay attention to
these words, and always be strong in faithful trust in well
being and in woe, for he loves us and delights in us, and so
he wishes us to love him and delight in him and trust
greatly in him, and all will be well.
(ST Ch 22)

Prayer for the world and for ourselves

Lord God, our refuge and our strength, a very present help
in trouble;
help us not to be afraid when the chaos around us and
within threatens to overwhelm us;
teach us to trust in your faithful love,
and sustain and refresh us with your grace,
for in you alone is our life. Amen.

Blessing

God's great goodness fills all his creatures
and all his blessed works full,
and endlessly overflows in them;
for he is everlastingness,
and he made us only for himself,
and restored us by his precious Passion.
May he always preserve us in his blessed love,
and all this of his goodness. Amen.

We go in the peace of Christ. Amen.

Suggested Words for Use at a Eucharist, reflecting Mother Julian's teaching

An act of Penitence
In our sight we do not stand,
in God's sight we do not fall.
Both these insights are true,
but the greater belongs to God.

Silence

Absolution
As by his courtesy God forgives our sins
when we repent, even so he wills
that we should forgive our sins,
and give up our senseless worrying
and faithless fear.

Collect
Mother, Father God, whose nature is
greater by far than we can imagine;
as we thank you for Mother Julian
and the insights she has given us,
in her *Revelation,*
we pray that you will draw us
to deeper understanding and love,
for the sake of Jesus Christ, our Lord.
Amen

Creed
God our Father, in you have our being
We praise and trust you.
God our Mother, from you came mercy and pity
We praise and trust you.
Holy Spirit, from you come grace and help,
We praise and trust you.
Holy God, Father, Son and Holy Spirit,
We praise and trust you.

Eucharistic Prayer
Lord God,
through your servant Julian
you revealed to us that
as Father you are all power and goodness,
and as Mother you are all wisdom and love;
We praise and glorify you.
We praise you that you hold
all creation in your love,
and enfold all creatures in your care;
We praise and glorify you.
With angels and archangels
And the whole company of heaven
We sing
Holy, holy, holy Lord,
God of life and love,
Heaven and earth are full of your glory,
All praise to your name.

Come to us now, Lord God
as we remember Jesus, who
on the night before he died,
took bread and wine, blessed them
and gave them to his friends, saying
This is my body, this is my blood.
Eat and drink to remember me.

Come to us now most courteous God,
and fill our hearts with longing for you;
God of your goodness, give us yourself.
Take from us all hesitancy and fear;
God of your goodness, give us yourself.
Draw us to delight in you, for you are
the God who longs for our love;
God of your goodness, give us yourself,
for we can ask for nothing less.
than that which can do you full worship.

If we ask anything less,
we shall always be in want.
Only in you we have all.
Amen

Blessing
God's goodness fills all his creatures
and all his blessed works full
and endlessly overflows in them;
for he is everlastingness,
and he made us only for himself,
and restored us by his precious Passion.
May he always preserve us in his blessed love,
and all this of his goodness. **Amen**

Suggestions for Further Reading

Revelations of Divine Love
Julian of Norwich
trans. Elizabeth Spearing
Penguin Classics 1998

Showings
Julian of Norwich
trans. E. Colledge and J.K. Walshe
Paulist Press 1978

Enfolded in Love
Daily readings
ed. Robert Llewelyn
DLT 1980

In Love Enclosed
Daily readings
ed. Robert Llewelyn
DLT 1985

Homely Love
Going on retreat with Julian of Norwich
Penny Roker
Canterbury Press 2006

Through Julian's Windows
Growing into wholeness with Julian of Norwich
Elizabeth Obbard
Canterbury Press 2008

The Book of Margery Kempe
trans. B.A. Windeatt
Penguin Classics 1985

Julian of Norwich
Grace Jantzen
SPCK 2000

In Search of Julian of Norwich
Sheila Upjohn
DLT 1989

With Pity not with Blame
Robert Llewelyn
DLT 1982

The Passion in Art
Richard Harries
Ashgate Publishing 2004

For more Information on Julian Meetings and Contemplative Prayer

Website: www.julianmeetings.org

Some Basics of Contemplative Prayer
The Julian Meetings

Starting a Julian meeting
The Julian Meetings

Circles of Stillness – Thoughts on Contemplative Prayer
ed. Hilary Wakeman
DLT 2002

Alexander Ryrie
Wonderful Exchange
Canterbury Press 2003